OWEN DAVEY

CRAZY ABOUT CATS

FLYING EYE BOOKS

London–New York

A very thirsty
Indochinese clouded
leopard.

CONTENTS

WHAT ARE CATS?

Cats are a group of mammals known scientifically as felids. Depending on which scientists you ask, there are between 37 to 41 different species. The house cat is very similar to wild cats in a lot of ways.

A puma exploring some wintery slopes.

Home Sweet Home

The type of place where an animal lives is called a habitat. Cats can live in a variety of habitats, from water-logged swamps and rainforests to sweltering deserts and even desolate snowscapes.

Nom Nom

Cats are obligate carnivores, which means that they have to eat meat in order to get the right nutrients for survival. Cats eat whatever they can get their paws on, including rodents, hares, birds, monkeys, antelopes, zebras, turtles, insects, deer, alligators, and snakes. Many will also hunt smaller species of cat.

Ocelots are sometimes eaten by larger cats.

The varied diet of cats.

Hard Cat to Follow

Cats tend to be shy of people. Many inhabit very remote areas, so we still have a lot to learn about some cat species.

Now that we know some of the basics, let's pounce into the wonderful world of wild cats, from the frozen mountains of Tibet to the grasslands of the Serengeti plain. Have you got your roar ready? It's time to go *Crazy About Cats*!

PAWS FOR THOUGHT

Felid-like animals have been around for roughly 50 million years, but modern wild cats began to evolve around 16 million years ago. Evolution is the process by which animals have changed over time. Certain characteristics are passed down from generation to generation that help them survive. Modern species of cat are split into 8 groups, based on their history of evolution.

Panthera Lineage
e.g. Tiger

Ocelot Lineage
e.g. Oncilla

Caracal Lineage
e.g. African golden cat

Bay Cat Lineage
e.g. Bay cat

Lynx Lineage
e.g. Eurasian lynx

Puma Lineage
e.g. Puma

Felis Lineage
e.g. Chinese mountain cat

Leopard Cat Lineage
e.g. Leopard cat

Domestication

House cats are some of the most popular pets in the world today, but the process of bringing moggies into our homes began many thousands of years ago. Recent studies suggest that cats started to live alongside humans between 9,000–10,000 years ago, around the time that humans began farming. Humans were growing and storing grains, which attracted large numbers of hungry rodents, and this rodent invasion in turn attracted wild cats. These wild cats became domesticated by hanging around humans to get easy food – and they provided efficient pest control at the same time.

This species of wild cat is imaginatively called a wildcat and is part of the Felis lineage.

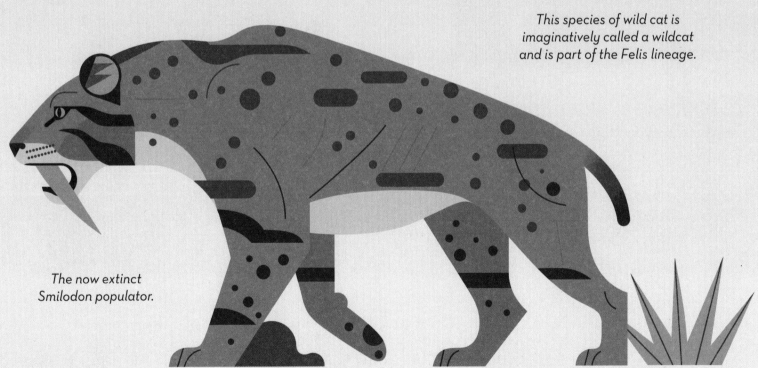

The now extinct Smilodon populator.

Tooth and Tail

Many felid species that once roamed the earth are now extinct. The prehistoric Smilodon populator, more commonly known as the sabre-toothed tiger, was built like a bear with huge knife-like teeth that were too big to fit in its mouth!

EAT, PREY, HUNT

Cats are some of the most successful carnivores on the planet.
Take a look at the real life super powers of this Asiatic golden cat.

Body

Cats have superb reflexes,
perfect balance, and flexible bodies.

*Falling cats twist their
bodies in mid-air to land on
their feet, like this kodkod.*

Tail

Tails help with balance
and are also used to
show emotions.

Whiskers

Also known as vibrissae, these
stiff hairs are so sensitive that
cats can use them to map their
surroundings by feeling the
movement of air around objects.

*Cats extend their claws by
tightening muscles and tendons.*

Claws

Cats' claws can be
hidden in their paws,
which helps to keep
them sharp.

Ears

Cats can detect far quieter and higher pitched sounds than us. Their ears rotate to pick up sounds from different locations.

Eyes

Cats' eyes have a mirror-like layer, called a tapetum lucidum, which reflects light and allows them to see amazingly well at night.

Noses

Cats have an excellent sense of smell. The ridges on their nose are as unique to each cat as a human fingerprint.

Teeth

The long, fang-like teeth are called canines, and are used for delivering precise killing bites to their prey.

Tongue

Covered in small curved spikes called filiform papillae, which are made of the same substance as our fingernails, cats' tongues work like a comb when they lick their fur.

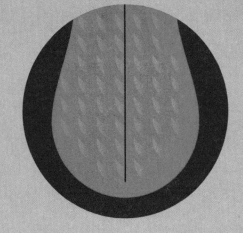

Paws

Soft pads on their toes allow cats to walk almost silently, so that they can sneak up on unaware prey.

Vomeronasal Organ

Found in the roof of a cat's mouth and used to detect smells produced by other cats (known as a scent).

HIDE AND SEEK

All wild cats are covered in fur, but the colour, pattern, and length of their coats can be very different. Each coat is unique to the cat and no two individuals have the same pattern.

Here are a few examples of the many beautiful patterns found on felids. Patterned cats usually live in jungles and forests, whilst cats with plain coloured fur generally live in more open areas like mountains and deserts.

'Camouflage' is when something blends in with its surroundings, making it hard to see. Being hidden is very useful for cats trying to keep out of sight of predators, or whilst hunting their prey.

Named because these markings look like roses, rosettes appear on several species. You can tell the difference between jaguars and leopards by looking for little black spots – these are only found inside the rosettes of a jaguar.

Jaguar rosette

Leopard rosettes

1

The marbled cat has beautiful cloud-like shapes with dark edges on the sides of its body. These copy the shapes of the sunlight that comes through the trees.

2

Tigers are the only cats with vertical stripes all over their bodies. In the wild they are remarkably well hidden when walking through long grass.

3

Like many small felids, this plain coloured pampas cat hides in open areas by flattening its body to the ground and staying very still.

Melanism is a term used to describe animals that are all black. The most famous is the black panther which is actually any black cat from the Panthera genus, most often leopards and jaguars. These cats hunt in dark forests where they can hide in the shadows.

4

If you look closely at this black leopard, you can still see the dark rosette markings in its fur.

5

The cheetah is well known for the small black spots all over its fur. These flecks help to break up the cat's outline, making it harder to see in the savannah.

HIGH LIFE

Featured Creatures: Margay

Margays are small cats that live in the rainforests of Central and South America. They look similar to ocelots and oncillas, but have larger eyes, a longer tail, and longer legs.

Branch Out

Their broad feet, sharp claws, long muscular tails, and flexible ankles (which can rotate 180 degrees), make these cats outstanding climbers. They move easily through treetops, leaping long distances between branches, sprinting head first down tree trunks and even hanging by their back legs!

Baby pied tamarin.

Copycat

Astonishingly, margays can copy the sounds of other animals in order to lure prey. One cat was heard making a noise similar to a baby tamarin monkey in order to encourage some adult monkeys to come closer.

Up All Night

Margays are nocturnal, which means they are more active at night-time. The dark provides better cover for hunting. Margays use their large super-powered eyes to see in the dark and sneak up on prey.

MAKING A MEAL OF THINGS

Many cats hunt alone, using their magnificent camouflage, power, and athleticism to catch prey. Tigers often wait by watering holes to attack the animals that come to drink, while snow leopards wait on ledges and surprise their prey by leaping onto them from above.

Snow leopard ready to pounce.

A fishing cat, doing what it does best.

Cats often use a technique known as stalking. They hide in the cover of grasses and hold their bodies close to the ground while moving slowly and quietly towards their prey. If the prey looks in their direction, the cat will freeze until it looks away again. When close enough, the cat sprints as fast as it can, leaps onto its prey and sinks its teeth into the neck or head to kill the animal.

The fishing cat uses its large webbed paws to hook fish out of the water. It will also dive head first into water to catch fish in its mouth.

Serval stalking its prey.

Leopard climbing a tree with a fresh kill.

To protect their food, many cats cover it with dirt, leaves, or snow, returning to feed for several days or even weeks in the winter. Leopards use their mouths to pull kills twice their own weight up into trees to avoid losing them to scavengers like lions and hyenas.

Jaguars are very versatile hunters and brilliant swimmers. They will sometimes float quietly downstream, looking for prey resting on the edge of the river.

This jaguar has caught a caiman in the river.

COMES WITH THE TERRITORY

Most adult cats live alone in an area known as their territory, which has everything they need to survive. Felids regularly communicate with each other in different ways to show who lives where.

Leave Your Mark

Every felid has glands on its cheeks, chin, forehead, feet, and tail, which are used to leave their scent around their territory. They also spray their wee on trees and rocks. Scent contains information about each cat, including age and gender. A cat must regularly go back and mark areas to let rivals know the place is still occupied. Many cats also scratch trees in their territory, which acts as an 'I was here' sign.

Two male bobcats scrapping over territory.

Cat Fight

If an unwelcome guest appears in another cat's territory, the two cats may hiss and growl or display their teeth to intimidate their opponent.
If nobody runs away, a fight may break out. Clashes of sharp claws and vicious biting can cause a lot of damage and occasionally lead to death. Older male cats are often heavily scarred from a lifetime of territorial battles.

Roar Deal

Felids can make many different noises, including growling, mewing, yelping, hissing, howling, and even whistling to talk to each other. Lions, tigers, leopards, and jaguars are the only cats that are able to roar. They use this long, deep, booming noise over great distances to warn other cats off their turf.

PRIDE AND PREDATORS

Featured Creatures: Lion

The most sociable of all the felids is the lion. They live in family groups known as prides, which may reach up to 50 individuals under the right conditions. These large cat societies were thought to have begun in order to protect their food. A group of lions can fight off scavengers far better than on their own.

Female prides of lionesses all raise their young together, and sometimes work together to bring down larger animals. Asian lions live in separate male and female prides and only come together during the mating season, but African lions stay together all year round.

A pride of lions, lounging about in the shade.

Mane Attraction

Adult males are easy to identify due to the long hair around their neck and chest, known as a mane, which is unique among the felids. It seems that lionesses prefer lions with longer, darker hair.

Male lions are capable of bringing down enormous prey by themselves. Lionesses are responsible for the majority of the hunting, but male lions always eat first. Young lion cubs are the last to eat.

The main job for male lions is to protect their territory from other gangs of males. They will usually be able to hold on to their territory for 2–4 years before being ousted by newcomers.

A black-haired male lion takes down a 1 tonne African buffalo.

AND THE AWARD GOES TO...

The loudest roar of all the cats belongs to the lion. Louder than a live rock band, this distinctive sound can be heard 5 miles away. One roaring lion can sometimes cause others to join in, forming a magnificent and fearsome chorus.

In relation to its body size, the Sunda clouded leopard has the largest canines of any living felid. These razor sharp teeth can reach 5 centimetres in length and are built to pierce skin. To accommodate their big teeth, these cats can open their mouths exceptionally wide when attacking prey.

The jaguar has the strongest jaws of all felids in relation to its size. Its immensely powerful bite can pierce the tough skin and skull of the caiman with ease, and it can even break the shells of turtles and tortoises.

Snow leopards have the longest tail of any cat compared to their overall size. During the cold winters, snow leopards curl their tails around themselves for warmth while they rest.

The record for the longest jump has to be shared between the snow leopard and the puma. Pumas can jump over 5 metres upwards into trees or onto ledges, but the snow leopard can jump over a 15 metre wide ditch. Between them, these awesome cats can jump the height and length of a double decker bus.

The odd prize for the most names goes to the puma. As well as puma, it is widely known as a cougar, mountain lion, and panther. Stranger names include catamount, shadow cat, deer tiger and mountain screamer.

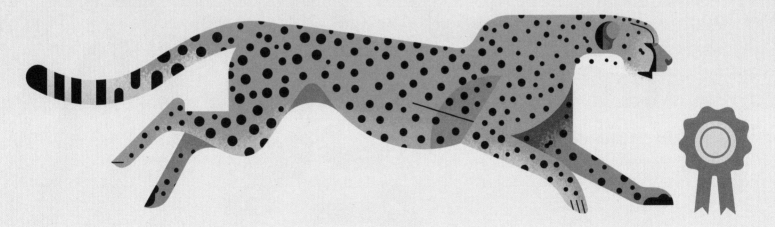

Cheetahs are the fastest animal on land. They can reach speeds of over 60 miles per hour in only a few seconds, and each stride takes them over 6 metres. Cheetahs have slim bodies, large nostrils to help them breathe, and ridges on their paws which act like the grip on car tires.

LITTLE AND LARGE

A life-size illustration of a rusty-spotted cat.

Featured Creatures:
Rusty-spotted cat

The adorable rusty-spotted cat looks very similar to house cats but is about half the size. Females can weigh as little as 1 kilogram: the same as a bag of sugar.

Despite their small stature, rusty-spotted cats are formidable hunters. Their speedy reflexes and agility mean that they can even catch birds in flight. Being small comes with disadvantages so these cats must often retreat up trees to hide from other predators.

Featured Creatures: Tiger

Tigers are the largest species of cat. Some wild males measure more than 3 metres long from head to tail, and weigh over 300 kilograms. These powerful striped beauties can take down animals several times their own weight, including huge and dangerous male gaurs.

A life-size illustration of a roaring tiger.

Gaurs are the largest wild cattle in the world.

Tigers live in a range of climates, from the freezing snow-covered mountains of the Amur region in Russia, to the humid mangrove swamps in Bangladesh. Amur tigers have thick fur and a layer of fat to keep them warm, and those in hotter regions often take refreshing dips in water to keep cool.

TO SCALE

Here you can see the size of some cats
compared to each other and humans.

Rusty-spotted cat

Southern tiger cat

Jungle cat

Eurasian lynx

Cheetah

1 metre

Leopard

Lion

Tiger

WEIRD AND WONDERFUL

Pallas' Cat

The fluffiest of all the wild felids. Its thick fur helps protect it from severely cold winters, which can drop below the temperature of a home freezer.

Serval

This big-eared beauty uses its excellent hearing to locate rodents and then performs a high arching pounce onto its oblivious prey.

Sand Cat

These oddballs live in deserts and have specialised furry feet to stop them from sinking into the soft sand.

Black-Footed Cat

These dinky felids have bands around their legs and are only a fraction larger on average than the rusty-spotted cat.

Iberian Lynx

The awesome facial hair of this cat is seen in both males and females and is technically known as a facial ruff. All lynxes have these short tails.

Caracal

Truly spectacular ear tufts! These cats were once kept by Indian rulers who would train them in pigeon-catching contests – the origin of the phrase 'cat among the pigeons'.

Jaguarundi

Believe it or not, this weasel-like creature is actually a cat. It hunts in the day and is regularly seen in Central and South America, but very little is known about it.

Flat-Headed Cat

An odd-looking creature that uses its partially webbed feet to feel for prey in shallow water.

KITTEN CABOODLE

Baby cats are known as kittens or cubs. A group born at the same time to the same mother are known as a litter. Cats tend to be excellent mothers and stay with their young for a long time, teaching them everything they need to survive.

Some cubs look quite different to their parents. Cheetah cubs have fluffy hair running along their spine which helps them blend into the grass. Pumas start life covered in spots, and lions are born with dark rosettes over their bodies which slowly fade.

Cheetah cub

Lion cub

Puma cub

Kittens and cubs are generally blind and deaf when they are first born, leaving them completely defenceless. The mother can carry her cubs to safety in between her teeth by grasping the loose skin on the back of the cub's neck.

Kittens drink their mothers' milk until they are old enough to eat meat. At first, mothers bring food to their cubs, but as the cubs grow up they begin to join in on hunts. Some mothers injure prey, leaving the cubs to work out what to do with it.

Canada lynx carrying her kitten.

Cats become better hunters by play-fighting. Using their mouths and paws, they learn the skills they need in order to tackle prey for themselves.

Geoffroy's cat kittens play-fighting.

CAT MYTHOLOGY

Cats have been feared and respected throughout much of human history. Before the days of online cat videos, many cultures told stories of cats in their folklore, mythology, and religions.

Mau

Ancient Egyptians really loved cats. Cats (known as mau) were connected with a number of Egyptian gods including the half-woman, half-cat goddess, Bastet, and the lioness-headed warrior goddess, Sekhmet. Killing a cat was punishable by death. Many mau were mummified and embalmed mice were put in their tombs, presumably so they could have food to eat in the afterlife.

Maneki-Neko

The beckoning cat (maneki-neko) is a common Japanese figure of a cat with one paw raised. It is believed to bring good luck to its owner. There are several tales about the origin of the maneki-neko, often involving a cat gesturing for someone to follow, leading to good luck, happiness or wealth.

Witchcraft

In the Middle Ages, people began to fear the practice known as 'witchcraft'. People believed that many animals, especially cats, were witches' helpers. Some even believed that witches rode on the backs of giant black house cats.

Nemean Lion

The Nemean lion was a legendary creature in Ancient Greek mythology. It had golden fur that could not be pierced by mortal weapons and claws sharp enough to cut through any armour. As part of his famous 'twelve labours', a mythical hero named Heracles killed the lion using his bare hands.

FELINE FINE

Sadly, over the last hundred years, many species of wild cat have become rare or endangered. As humans take up more and more of the planet, we are destroying natural habitats and forcing cats to live closer to our communities and farmland.

Endangered Andean mountain cats are sometimes killed by local people in Patagonia and Argentina.

Many felids hunt livestock because they are easy prey. Some herders choose to protect their animals by illegally hunting the local wild cats and selling their fur and body parts.

There are ways to prevent these attacks in the first place, including providing farmers with better fencing. Ranchers in Argentina have begun using livestock-guarding dogs as defence against predators.

Livestock-guarding dogs.

Ecotourism can also help to protect wild cats and increase profits for local people. The most popular attractions on safari tours are often cats. Protected lands like these provide felids with areas in which to thrive.

A lucky ecotourist's view of a famously shy snow leopard.

If you want to help protect these magnificent creatures and their habitats, you can look for the FSC® label and Rainforest Alliance Certified™ seal when you shop. These help to ensure that a product has been grown and harvested using environmentally and socially responsible practices.

INDEX

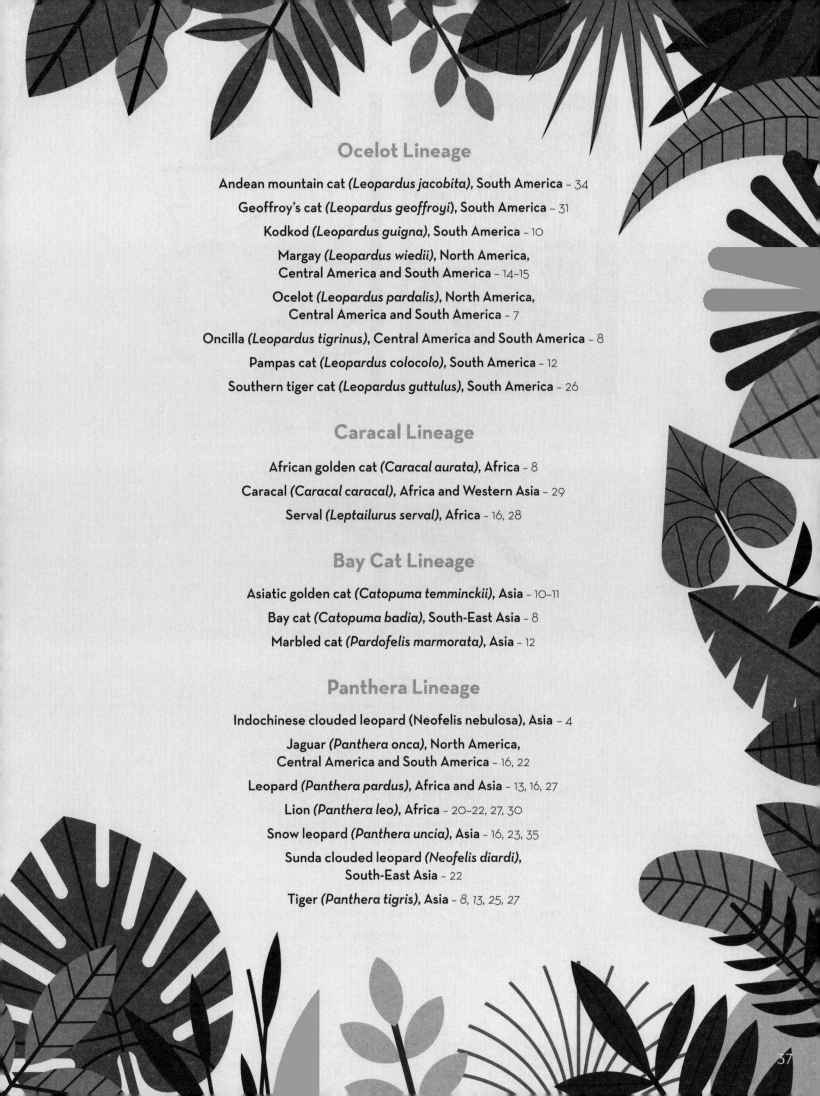

Ocelot Lineage

Andean mountain cat *(Leopardus jacobita)*, South America – 34

Geoffroy's cat *(Leopardus geoffroyi)*, South America – 31

Kodkod *(Leopardus guigna)*, South America – 10

Margay *(Leopardus wiedii)*, North America,
Central America and South America – 14–15

Ocelot *(Leopardus pardalis)*, North America,
Central America and South America – 7

Oncilla *(Leopardus tigrinus)*, Central America and South America – 8

Pampas cat *(Leopardus colocolo)*, South America – 12

Southern tiger cat *(Leopardus guttulus)*, South America – 26

Caracal Lineage

African golden cat *(Caracal aurata)*, Africa – 8

Caracal *(Caracal caracal)*, Africa and Western Asia – 29

Serval *(Leptailurus serval)*, Africa – 16, 28

Bay Cat Lineage

Asiatic golden cat *(Catopuma temminckii)*, Asia – 10–11

Bay cat *(Catopuma badia)*, South-East Asia – 8

Marbled cat *(Pardofelis marmorata)*, Asia – 12

Panthera Lineage

Indochinese clouded leopard *(Neofelis nebulosa)*, Asia – 4

Jaguar *(Panthera onca)*, North America,
Central America and South America – 16, 22

Leopard *(Panthera pardus)*, Africa and Asia – 13, 16, 27

Lion *(Panthera leo)*, Africa – 20–22, 27, 30

Snow leopard *(Panthera uncia)*, Asia – 16, 23, 35

Sunda clouded leopard *(Neofelis diardi)*,
South-East Asia – 22

Tiger *(Panthera tigris)*, Asia – 8, 13, 25, 27

If you like this, you'll love...

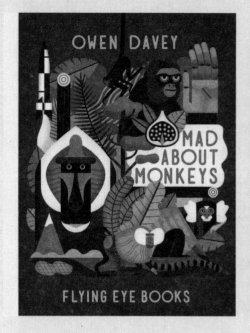

978-1-909263-57-4

978-1-909263-91-8

To the cubs in my life: Max, Oliver, Henry and Alyssia.

Crazy About Cats is © Flying Eye Books 2017.

This is a first edition published in 2017 by Flying Eye Books,
an imprint of Nobrow Ltd. 27 Westgate Street, London E8 3RL.

Text and illustrations © Owen Davey 2017.
Consultant: Dr Nick Crumpton
Owen Davey has asserted his right under the Copyright,
Designs and Patents Act, 1988, to be identified
as the Author and Illustrator of this Work.

Published in the US by Nobrow (US) Inc.
Printed in Latvia on FSC® certified paper.

ISBN: 978-1-911171-16-4
Order from www.flyingeyebooks.com